BENJAMIN GODARD
Suite de Trois Morceaux

for flute and piano

Editor: Trevor Wye

1 Allegretto
2 Idylle
3 Valse

CHESTER MUSIC

Suite de Trois Morceaux
1 ALLEGRETTO

BENJAMIN GODARD

Op.116

CH 55136

2 IDYLLE

3 VALSE

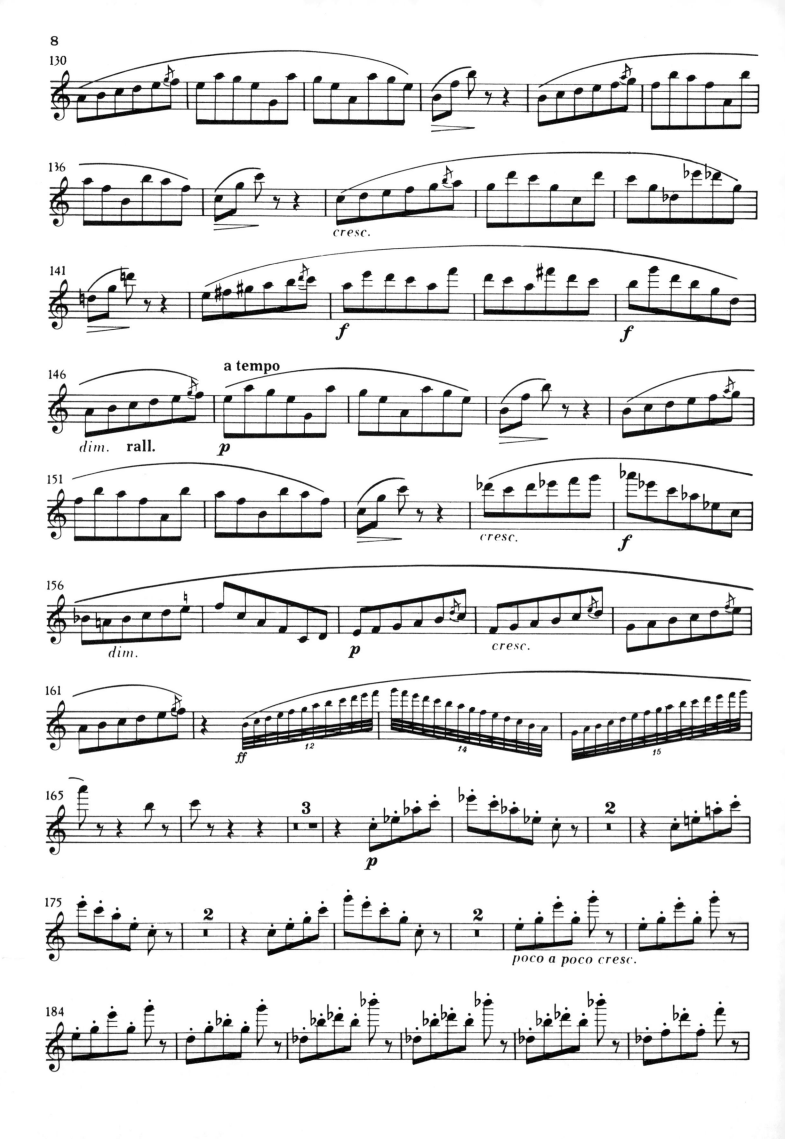

SELECTED MUSIC FOR FLUTE AND KEYBOARD

J.C. BACH	Sonata Op. 18 No. 1
J.S. BACH	Book 1: Sonatas Nos: 1-3
J.S. BACH	Book 2: Sonatas Nos: 4-6
BENTZON	Variations on an Original Theme
BERKELEY	Concerto (with Piano Reduction)
BERKELEY	Sonata
COOPER	Sonata for Flutes
DOPPLER	Hungarian Pastoral Fantasy Op. 26
FAURE	Fantasie Op. 79
FAURE	Sicilienne
LE FLEMING	Air and Dance
GENIN	Carnival of Venice Op. 14
GODARD	Suite de Trois Morceaux
HOVLAND	Suite
B. KELLY	Sonatina
KREBS	Sonata in A Major
KVANDAL	Romance
MACONCHY	Colloquy
MAW	Sonatina
NIELSEN	The Fog is Lifting
OSWALD	Airs for the Seasons
POULENC	Sonata
POWNING	Vegetable Suite
SCOTT	Scotch Pastoral
STANLEY	Six Solos Op. 4
TELEMANN	Sonata in B Minor
VIVALDI	Sonata in C

SOLO FLUTE

BENTZON	Variations Op. 93
BERGE	Flute Solo
DEBUSSY	Syrinx
MORTENSEN	Sonata Op. 6
NIELSEN	The Children are Playing
SOMMERFELDT	Divertimento
WESTERGAARD	Sonata

STUDIES

ANDERSEN	24 Short Studies Op. 33
ANDERSEN	100 Posthumous Studies
ANDERSEN	26 Small Caprices Op. 37
ANDERSEN	24 Technical Studies Op. 63
BOEHM	24 Capriccios
KÖHLER	Progress in Flute Playing Book 1 Op. 33
KÖHLER	Progress in Flute Playing Book 2 Op. 33
KÖHLER	Progress in Flute Playing Book 3 Op. 33

from

CHESTER MUSIC

| Flute | Editor: Trevor Wye | | Clarinet | Editor: Thea King |
| Oboe | Editor: James Brown | | Bassoon | Editor: William Waterhouse |

Saxophone   Editor: Paul Harvey

A growing collection of volumes from Chester Music, containing a
wide range of pieces from different periods.

FLUTE SOLOS VOLUME I

Baston	Siciliana from Concertino in D
Blavet	Gavotte—La Dédale
Bochsa	Nocturne
Buchner	Russian Melody from Fantasy op. 22
Eichner	Minuet from Sonata No. 6
Franck	Intrada
Franck	Galliard
Lichtenthal	Theme
Mozart	Minuets I & II from Sonata No. 1
Paisiello	Nel Cor Più
Vivaldi	Andante from Sonata No. 3 of The Faithful Shepherd
Vivaldi	Pastorale from Sonata No. 4 of The Faithful Shepherd

FLUTE SOLOS VOLUME II

Blavet	Les Tendres Badinages from Sonata No. 6
Chopin	A Rossini Theme
Donjon	Adagio Nobile
Eichner	Scherzando from Sonata No. 6
Harmston	Andante
Jacob	Cradle Song from Five Pieces for Harmonica and Piano
Mozart	Minuets I & II from Sonata No. 5
Mozart	Allegro from Sonata in G
Pauli	Capriccio
Telemann	Tempo Giusto from Sonata in D minor
Vivaldi	Allegro from Sonata No. 6 of The Faithful Shepherd

FLUTE SOLOS VOLUME III

Blavet	Sicilienne from Sonata No. 4	Loeillet	Gavotte and Aria from Sonata No. 7
Blavet	Les Regrets from Sonata No. 5	Nørgard	Andantino—Pastorale
Donjon	Offertoire op. 12	Sibelius	Solo from Scaramouche op. 71
Eichner	Allegro from Sonata No. 6	Telemann	Grave from Sonata in G minor
Kelly	Jig from Serenade	Vivaldi	Largo from Sonata No. 6 of The Faithful Shepherd

Also available: FLUTE DUETS AND TRIOS

Further details on request

CHESTER MUSIC
(A division of Music Sales Limited)
8/9 Frith Street, London W1V 5TZ
Exclusive distributors: Music Sales Limited
Newmarket Road, Bury St. Edmunds, Suffolk IP33 3YB

BENJAMIN GODARD
Suite de Trois Morceaux

for flute and piano

Editor: Trevor Wye

1 Allegretto
2 Idylle
3 Valse

CHESTER MUSIC

Suite de Trois Morceaux
1 ALLEGRETTO

BENJAMIN GODARD

Op. 116

2 IDYLLE

3 VALSE

16

273

279

poco a poco più mosso

285

poco a poco più mosso

291

Printed and bound in Great Britain by
Caligraving Limited Thetford Norfolk

6/04 (51478)